£3.95

©1989 GRANDREAMS LIMITED

Written by *Tony Lynch*,

Layout and design by
The Character Licensing Illustration Company.

Photographs supplied by:
All Sport pages 6, 7, 18 (bottom), 19, 22, 31 (bottom), 35, 39
(bottom right), 40, 41, 44 (top), 45, 50, 51, 52, 53, 54, 55, 56.
Syndication International pages 16, 17, 20, 21 (bottom), 24
(bottom), 25, 26, 27, 28, 29, 30. *All Action Photographic*
pages 2, 3, 11, 18 (top), 23, 31 (top), 32, 33, 36, 37, 44
(bottom), 48, 49, 58, 59, 60. *Associated Sports Photography*
pages 8, 9, 10, 12, 13, 21 (top), 24 (top) 38, 39 (top x 2 and
bottom left), 42, 43, 47.

Published by

GRANDREAMS LIMITED
Jadwin House, 205-211 Kentish Town Road,
London, NW5 2JU.

Printed in Italy

ISBN 0 86227 677 2

All information correct at time of going to press.

CONTENTS

LIVERPOOL'S ROLL OF HONOUR

League Champions:
*1900-01, 1905-06, 1921-22, 1922-23, 1946-47,
1963-64, 1965-66, 1972-73, 1975-76, 1976-77,
1978-79, 1979-80, 1981-82, 1982-83, 1983-84,
1985-86, 1987-88.*

League Runners-up:
*1898-99, 1909-10, 1968-69, 1973-74, 1974-75,
1977-78, 1984-85, 1986-87, 1988-89.*

Division Two Champions:
1893-94, 1895-96, 1904-05, 1961-62.

FA Cup Winners:
1965, 1974, 1986, 1989.

FA Cup Runners-up:
1914, 1950, 1971, 1977, 1988.

**Football League Cup (later Milk Cup,
now Littlewoods Cup) Winners:**
1981, 1982, 1983, 1984.
Runners-up:
1978, 1987.

European Cup Winners:
1976-77, 1977-78, 1980-81, 1983-84.
Runners-up:
1984-85.

**European Cup Winners' Cup
Runners-up:**
1965-66.

UEFA Cup Winners:
1972-73, 1975-76.

European Super Cup Winners:
1977.

**World Club Championship
Runners-up:**
1981.

The superb record of Liverpool Football Club speaks for itself. Winning the Football League no less than a record 17 times makes Liverpool the single most successful side that English soccer has ever produced.

In addition Liverpool has won the FA Cup four times, the League Cup (Littlewoods Cup) four times, the European Cup four times and the UEFA Cup twice.

No wonder the red scarfed, red hatted fans on Anfield's famous Kop have a lot to shout about! Consistency is the hallmark of Liverpool's style. And these days, under the expert guidance of manager Kenny Dalglish, the club is always striving to improve on past glories.

In 1988, when The Reds were powering towards that 17th Championship, the ex-England international winger Tom Finney (one of the finest footballers of all time) was moved to state that Liverpool were "...the best team of all time". This book sets out to celebrate that fact.

We hope you enjoy it...

LIVERPOOL
SEASON REVIEW
1988~89

Having come so close to the elusive League and Cup 'double' in 1987-88, Liverpool began the '88-89 determined to have another crack at football's 'mission impossible'.

In '87-88 The Reds had dominated the English First Division from start to finish with a magnificent display of consistency - there was little doubt that they would win the Championship. And they did so with a commanding 9 points margin over closest rivals Manchester United.

Liverpool had looked odds-on favourites to win the 1988 FA Cup, too. But Final opponents, Wimbledon, were to prove that football really is an unpredictable game, by defeating the mighty Reds 1-0 - with a Lawrie Sanchez goal in the 37th minute.

Liverpool's 1988-89 season was to curiously mirror that of the previous year. Sadly, it was also to be a season marred by terrible tragedy.

Amazingly, mainly due to injury problems, Liverpool did not look at all like Championship challengers throughout the first half of the League campaign.

Indeed, for a long while it looked as if a revitalised Norwich City would walk away with the title and so become the pride of Norfolk. Arsenal, too, were putting in a strong bid for the Championship on behalf of north London.

In mid-December, Liverpool lost at home to Norwich and then suffered a 1-3 defeat to Manchester United on New Year's Day. Many pundits saw this as the writing on the wall and the beginning of the end for Kenny Dalglish's Red Army.

But, of course, the pundits have written-off Liverpool before, and have usually been forced to eat their words.

In fact, that turn-of-the-year defeat by United was to prove a turning point in Liverpool's season. From then on they did not look

John Aldridge scores Liverpool's second goal in their 3-1 win over Nottingham Forerst in the semi-final of the FA Cup.

back and began to play in the style of the previous season. Even so, the task of catching the League leaders was an enormous one.

By March 19, The Reds were in eighth position and 19 points adrift of leaders Arsenal. But two months later the gap had narrowed to a mere two points with Liverpool in second place, following a run of superb form.

But then, however, tragedy had struck.

As everyone now knows, the disaster at Hillsborough, home of Sheffield Wednesday, occurred on April 15th, 1989 just six minutes after the start of Liverpool's FA Cup semi-final against Nottingham Forest.

Ninety-five football fans lost their lives in the terrible crush at the Leppings Lane end of the ground.

News of the disaster stunned the world, and in its sad aftermath, came an overwhelming outpouring of emotion by the people of Liverpool. Fans brought their tributes - wreaths, flowers, scarves and other mementos - into Anfield, and the ground became a shrine to the memory of those who had died. It was the most moving sight football has ever seen.

Liverpool Football Club now had to pull itself together. For a while there was talk of the team pulling out of the FA Cup competition altogether. Eventually, however, the decision

was taken, quite rightly, to continue.

Liverpool's first match after the disaster was a fund raising game against Celtic. This was followed by the resumption of the League programme with fittingly, a local derby against Everton, at Goodison Park. In the event, the 0-0 score line hardly mattered. More importantly the match did much to restore the morale on Merseyside.

The rearranged semi-final with Nottingham Forest was played at Old Trafford, home of Manchester United. In an emotionally-charged game Liverpool notched up a resounding 3-1 victory, with two goals from John Aldridge and an own goal by Forest's Brian Laws.

The Reds were in the FA Cup Final for the

Above: The Shankly Gates with some of the tributes from fans for the 95 who died at Hillsborough. Opposite page right: Arsenal's Michael Thomas scores in the very last seconds in their match against Liverpool which decided the fate of the First Division Championship.

ninth time in their history. Their opponents on this occasion were neighbours Everton, making the match only the second-ever 'Merseyside Cup Final'.

At Wembley Liverpool's top scorer, John Aldridge, put The Reds ahead with his first touch of the ball, after only four minutes. From then on a dour battle ensued as Everton tried hard to find an equaliser.

But this was to be a game dominated by two SuperSubs.

In the 58th minute The Blues brought on substitute Stuart McCall, in place of Paul Bracewell. The fiery redhead seemed to revitalise Everton and it was fitting that McCall should score the 90th minute equaliser, in a goalmouth scramble, and take the match into extra-time.

John Aldridge had been substituted by Ian Rush in the 72nd minute. And Rushie was destined to make his mark on the match. In the fifth minute of extra-time he collected a pass for Steve Nicol, turned past the Everton skipper, Kevin Ratcliffe, and fired a terrific shot past Neville Southall - making the score line 2-1 to Liverpool.

But Everton weren't giving up as easily as that. Seven minutes later, the excitement rose even higher when McCall volleyed in his second equaliser of the game: 2-2.

But it was Ian Rush who would have the last word by heading in the match-winner in the 104th minute (in the process he beat Dixie Dean's record of 19 goals scored in Liverpool-Everton derbies).

And so captain Ronnie Whelan collected the FA Cup from the Duchess of Kent - and once again the 'double' looked a distinct possibility.

In the wake of the Hillsborough disaster Liverpool's League programme had been unavoidably and understandably delayed, and a backlog of fixtures had to be played.

After the local derby League game against Everton and the rearranged semi-final against Nottingham Forest, Liverpool played Forest at Anfield in a League match. The Reds won 1-0, thanks to a John Aldridge penalty.

Liverpool's next opponents were Wimbledon, the little London club who were determined to have a say in the outcome of the title race. But the plucky Dons were unable to repeat their Wembley giant-killing act of the previous May. The Reds won 2-1, with goals from John Aldridge and John Barnes. On that same Saturday - May 13 - League leaders Arsenal lost 1-2 at home to Derby County, thereby making the title race well and truly open.

A 2-2 draw between Arsenal and Wimbledon and victories by

Liverpool over Queens Park Rangers (2-0) and West Ham United (5-1) brought the League Championship to a magnificent climax.

Arsenal were to play Liverpool at Anfield in the last game of the season, on Friday May 26. The Gunners had to win by a two goal margin to clinch the title - anything less and the League trophy would stay in the Anfield boardroom, and the 'double' would belong to Liverpool for the second time in four seasons.

It was to prove a tough match, played on a knife-edge of nerves.

A goalless first half made for even keener tension in the second. And when Alan Smith headed Arsenal into a 1-0 lead in the 52nd minute the stage was set for a thrilling end to the season. Liverpool had to hold on, Arsenal had to score one more.

The tension was

relieved in the very last minute of the game when Arsenal's Michael Thomas latched onto a rebound off Gary Ablett and scored the Gunners's second. Shortly afterwards the final whistle sounded and Arsenal were Champions.

The Gunners collected the trophy to resounding applause - everyone at Anfield that night knew they had seen a great game and a stirring performance by Arsenal.

Liverpool had stumbled and fallen at the last hurdle before the elusive 'double'. Yet, in a season dominated by trauma and grief, The Reds had achieved a remarkable record: FA Cup winners and League Runners-up.

It is certain that Liverpool Football Club will be chasing the highest honours in 1989-90, and that their players and fans will never walk alone.

FA CUP FINAL
PICTURE SPECIAL

Everton v. Liverpool. Played at Wembley, 20th May, 1989.

Opposite page top left: John Aldridge scores for Liverpool after just four minutes. *This page below left*: Substitute Stuart McCall equalises for Everton in the last seconds of normal time. *This page below right*: Liverpool go 2-1 up thanks to a superbly volleyed goal by Ian Rush. *Opposite page bottom right*: It's all square again as Bruce Grobbelaar is beaten by McCall's shot. *This page above*: From John Barnes' cross, Ian Rush heads home the winner, then turns to acknowledge Barnes' congratulations. *Opposite page far side*: Captain Ronnie Whelan with the FA Cup.

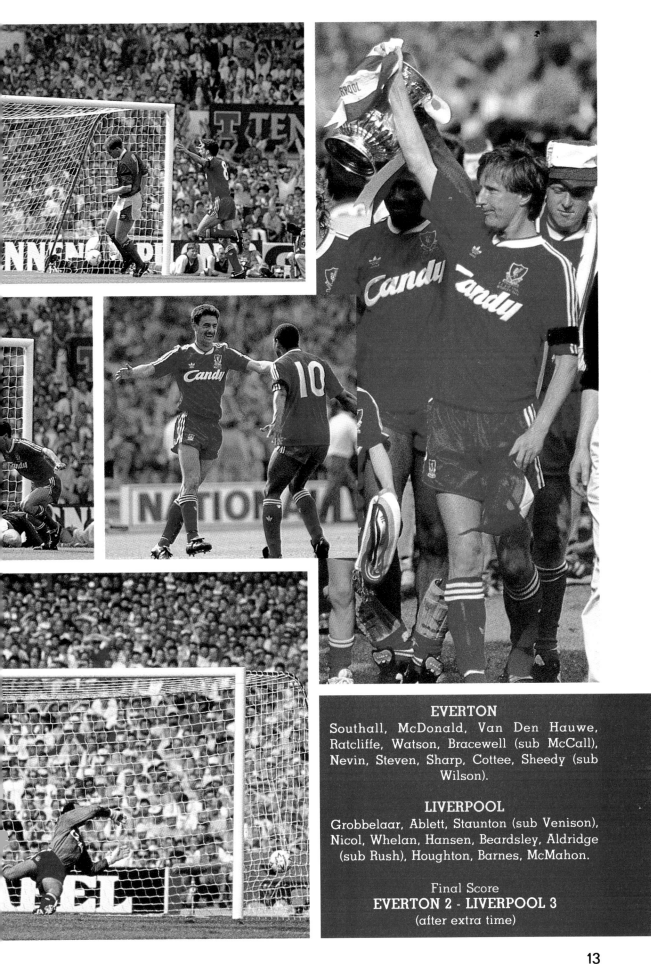

EVERTON
Southall, McDonald, Van Den Hauwe, Ratcliffe, Watson, Bracewell (sub McCall), Nevin, Steven, Sharp, Cottee, Sheedy (sub Wilson).

LIVERPOOL
Grobbelaar, Ablett, Staunton (sub Venison), Nicol, Whelan, Hansen, Beardsley, Aldridge (sub Rush), Houghton, Barnes, McMahon.

Final Score
EVERTON 2 - LIVERPOOL 3
(after extra time)

LIVERPOOL-A CHRONOLOGY

1870
Consecration of the Chapel of St. Domingos, Breckfield Road North, in the Everton district of Liverpool.

1878
St. Domingo Football Club is founded.

1879
The club's name is changed to Everton Football Club, they play on an open pitch in Stanley Park.

1880
Everton joins the Lancashire Association League.

1882
The Lancashire Association rules that its clubs must play on enclosed grounds. Everton find a suitable ground in Priory Road.

1884
The club moves yet again to a new ground called Anfield.

1885
Professionalism is introduced into English football.

1888
Everton become founder members of the Football League.

1892
A dispute over the rental of Anfield results in Everton leaving the ground and forming a new club at Goodison Park. John Houlding forms a new club at Anfield. Its name: Liverpool Football Club. John McKenna is appointed Liverpool's first manager. The club's application to join the Second Division is turned down and they join the Lancashire League. Liverpool's first game is played, against Rotherham - Liverpool win 7-1.

1893
Liverpool are accepted as a member of the Football League's Second Division.

1894
Liverpool win the Division Two title without losing a single game. A 'test match' victory over Newton Heath (later to become Manchester United) sees them promoted to the First Division.

1895
Liverpool are relegated to Division Two after just one season in the top flight.

1896
Liverpool become Second Division Champions for the second time.

1899
Liverpool reach the semi-finals of the FA Cup, but lose to Sheffield United after three replays.

1901
Liverpool become Football League Champions for the first time.

1904
Relegated to the Second Division.

1905
Division Two Champions for the third time.

1906
Liverpool become Football League Champions for the second time.

1914
FA Cup Runners-up to Burnley (0-1). The match, played at the Crystal Palace ground in London, is attended by between 72,000 and 100,000 spectators, among them King George V, the first reigning monarch to watch an FA Cup Final.

1922
Liverpool become Football League Champions for the third time.

1923
Football League Champions for the fourth time.

1947
Football League Champions for the fifth time.

1950
FA Cup Runners-up to Arsenal (0-2) at Wembley.

1954
They finish the season 22nd in Division One and are relegated to the Second.

1962
Revitalised under the management of Bill Shankly, Liverpool become Second Division Champions for the fourth time.

1964
Liverpool become Football League Champions for the sixth time.

1965
Liverpool win the FA Cup for the first time in their history, beating Leeds United 2-1 after extra time. They reach the semi-final of the European Cup, but lose by a 3-4 aggregate to Inter Milan.

1966
Football League Champions for the seventh time. Runners-up in the European Cup Winners' Cup, 1-2 to Borussia Dortmund at Hampden Park.

1971
FA Cup Runners-up, losing 1-2 to Arsenal after extra time.

1973
Football League Champions for the eighth time. UEFA Cup Winners, beating Borussia Moenchengladbach 3-2 on aggregate.

1974
FA Cup Winners, beating Newcastle United 3-0. Bill Shankly retires. He is succeeded by Bob Paisley.

1976
Football League Champions for the ninth time. UEFA Cup Winners, beating FC Bruges 4-3 on aggregate.

1977
Football League Champions for the tenth time. FA Cup Runners-up to Manchester United (1-2). European Cup Winners, beating Borussia Moenchengladbach 3-1 in Rome.

1978
European Cup Winners, beating FC Bruges 1-0 at Wembley. League Cup Runners-up to Nottingham Forest.

1979
Football League Champions for the eleventh time.

1980
Football League Champions for the twelfth time.

1981
European Cup Winners, beating Real Madrid 1-0 in Paris.

1982
Football League Champions for the thirteenth time. Football League Cup Winners, beating Tottenham Hotspur 3-1 after extra time.

1983
Football League Champions for the fourteenth time. Milk Cup Winners, beating Manchester United 2-1 after extra time. Bob Paisley retires, having become the most successful manager of an English football team. He is succeeded by Joe Fagan.

1984
Football League Champions for the fifteenth time. Milk Cup Winners, beating Everton 1-0 after a replay. European Cup Winners, beating AS Roma on penalties after a 1-1 draw, in Rome.

1985
European Cup Runners-up, losing 0-1 to Juventus in Brussels. Joe Fagan retires. He is succeeded by Kenny Dalglish.

1986
'Double' winners. Football League Champions for the sixteenth time, and FA Cup Winners for the third time, beating Everton 3-1.

1988
Football League Champions for the seventeenth time. FA Cup Runners-up, losing 0-1 to Wimbledon.

1989
FA Cup Winners for fourth time beating Everton 3-1 after extra time. Football League Runners-up. Miss second 'double' on goal difference.

GREAT GAMES II

LIVERPOOL v. LEEDS

FA Cup Final
Played at Wembley Stadium
1st May, 1965.

Twice before Liverpool had reached the FA Cup Final, and twice before they had lost at the last stage; in 1914, Burnley had beaten them 1-0, and 36 years later, in 1950, Arsenal had put on a devastating display to emerge as 2-0 victors.

Would the Reds be lucky at the third attempt?

By now Liverpool were considered a potent force in English football. Under the shrewd management of Bill Shankly they had risen from the depths of the Second Division in 1961-62 to win the League Championship just two years later. In 1965 they had finished the League season in 7th position while Cup Final opponents

Leeds United had finished as Runners-up to Manchester United.

So, it was a pretty evenly matched set of players who strode out onto Wembley's hallowed turf on that unusually dull afternoon in May, 1965. The weather may have been grey, but the famous old stadium was awash with the red of Liverpool and the white of Leeds.

Gerry Byrne.

The game got off to a dramatic start when, within five minutes, 'Pool's Gerry Byrne was involved in a collision with United's Bobby Collins. Byrne suffered a broken collar bone and was taken off the field, protesting that he wanted to continue playing.

This was in the days before substitutes were allowed in English football, so Liverpool were down to ten men - at least for the time being.

Liverpool's 'hero' Gerry Byrne tussles with Leeds Willie Bell.

Incredibly, after a spot of dressing room treatment Gerry Byrne was able to carry on! Despite what must have been an agonising injury the brave Byrne was as fearless as ever, putting in tackle after tackle in what was becoming an increasingly physical tie.

The game was, in fact, dominated by the two defences - considered the best in the country. Ron Yeats was magnificent for Liverpool at one end - and his endeavours were matched by the towering Jack Charlton at the other.

And so, after 90 minutes the score line remained at 0-0. It was the first time in 18 years that extra time was required in an FA Cup Final.

Three minutes into extra time and Liverpool went ahead, through Roger Hunt. This lead was wiped out eight minutes later when Billy Bremner scored the equaliser for Leeds.

By now the excitement was intense. It was anyone's game.

The stalemate was broken in the second period of extra time, when

Liverpool's Ian Callaghan crossed a beautifully weighted ball into the path of Ian St. John.

'The Saint' launched himself into the air to head home the most important goal of his distinguished career.

Liverpool held on for the remainder of the match to win the FA Cup for the first time in their long history.

On the team's return to Merseyside they were greeted by tumultuous applause and cheering as the Liverpool faithful lined the streets between Lime Street Station and the Town Hall where a magnificent reception was held.

Right: Liverpool celebrate at the end of the match. Below: Liverpool's two goalscorers, Ian St. John(left), and Roger Hunt.

Leeds United:
Sprake, Reaney, Bell, Bremner, Charlton, Hunter, Giles, Storrie, Peacock, Collins, Johanneson.

Liverpool:
Lawrence, Lawler, Byrne, Strong, Yeats, Stevenson, Callaghan, Hunt, St.John, Smith, Thompson.

Final Score:
LEEDS UNITED 1 - LIVERPOOL 2

Ian rush back at Liverpool after only one season away.

RUSH'S RETURN

The summer of 1988 brought some great news for Liverpool fans - it was announced that Ian Rush, the 'Goal Machine' was returning to Anfield, his happiest hunting ground, for a reputed transfer fee of £2.8 million.

Rush had been sold to Juventus, in Italy, for a massive £3.2 million in June 1987.

Although it was quite obvious that he was decidedly unhappy in his first season in the Italian League, it was expected that he would remain there for a few more seasons at least.

Of course, every English manager, with money to spend, was hoping that 'Rushie' would express a wish to return to England at some time in the near future. But the swiftness of Kenny Dalglish's transfer swoop took everyone by surprise.

Rush had hardly had time to say "Ciao Turin," before he was saying "Hello again, Liverpool."

Ian Rush - one of the greatest goalscorers of all time - was born in St. Asaph, Flint, North Wales, on 20 October, 1961. As a small child he suffered from the dangerous disease meningitis - but thankfully he recovered to become a fine young footballer.

In 1979 he became an apprentice player with Third Division

Below and opposite page: Ian Rush in the Juventus colours.

Chester City. He played 34 games for the 'Blues' and scored 14 goals. In April 1980 he was snapped up by Liverpool's manager Bob Paisley for £300,000.

It took Ian a while to settle in at Anfield. He

made just 9 appearances in his first season with the club (1980-81) and failed to score on each occasion.

But the 1981-82 season saw a transformation in the lad. His goal touch returned and he scored 30 times in 49 League and Cup appearances. After that his

consistently good finishing made him the most feared striker in the Football League. Before his move to Juventus, Rush had made 320 appearances for Liverpool and had scored a staggering 198 goals.

His stay in Italy was to prove a disappointing one (as so many British players have found). His natural game was stifled by the cloying, clogging defences that dominate

the Italian League. There were language and cultural problems too - and Ian felt decidedly unhappy about the whole situation.

The move had been a mistake.

And it was Kenny Dalglish who nipped in, before anyone else had a chance, to bring Rushie back to Anfield where he was welcomed with open arms by team-mates and fans alike.

GREAT GAMES 2

LIVERPOOL v. INTER MILAN

European Cup Semi-Final
(first leg)
Played at Anfield
4th May, 1965.

night. Following a well worked free-kick Ian Callaghan scored Liverpool's second goal after 34 minutes.

A few nervy moments in the second half, when Liverpool almost conceded two own-goals, were soon forgotten when Ian St. John scored the team's third goal.

But despite the 3-1 first-leg margin, Liverpool were not destined to become the first English club to win the **European Cup** (that honour would fall to Manchester United three years later). The second leg in Milan proved a highly suspect affair, with Inter winning 3-0, for a 4-3 aggregate victory. The Italian team went on to win the trophy, beating Benfica of Portugal 1-0.

Just three days after winning the 1965 FA Cup Final, Liverpool were involved in another big match. This time their opponents were Inter Milan of Italy. The occasion was the first leg Semi-Final of the European Cup. The Reds were ambitious to add to a glorious season by becoming the first English club to lift that famous trophy.

The match was a sell-out with Anfield's gates closed two hours before the kick-off.

Before the game started Gerry Byrne and Gordon Milne, two injured heroes of the Wembley win, paraded the FA Cup in front of Liverpool's adoring fans.

And so, by the time the game began, the excitement inside Anfield was at fever pitch.

Inter Milan, somewhat jarred by the atmosphere, were a little shaky. Liverpool were quick to capitalise on this factor and went ahead after only four minutes through Roger Hunt.

Mazzola equalised for the Italians shortly afterwards. But nothing was going to quell the Red Fever on this

Liverpool's three goalscorers: Left: *Roger Hunt.* Top: *Ian Callaghan and above:* Ian *St. John scoring his team's third goal.*

Liverpool:
Lawrence, Lawler, Moran, Strong, Yeats, Stevenson, Callaghan, Hunt, St.John, Smith, Thompson.

Inter Milan:
Sarti, Burgnich, Facchetti, Tagnin, Guarneri, Picchi, Jair, Mazzola, Piero, Suarez, Corso.

Final Score:
LIVERPOOL 3 - INTER MILAN 1

SUPER
RED
John Barnes

22

SUPER RED

John Aldridge

GREAT GAMES 3

LIVERPOOL v. EVERTON

League Division One
Played at Anfield
21st November, 1970.

Steve Heighway who scored Liverpool's first goal.

the first flush of success, which had seen The Reds rise from the Second Division with players like Gordon Milne, Ron Yeats, Ian St. John, Roger Hunt, Jimmy Melia and Gerry Byrne.

Most of these players had gone to pastures new and 'Shanks' was now reliant on a new squad of youngsters, including university graduates Brian Hall and Steve Heighway, goalkeeper Ray Clemence, forward Alun Evans and newcomer John Toshack signed for a club record of £110,000 from Cardiff City. This squad was backed by the experience of Liverpool's greatest servant, Ian Callaghan.

But the Liverpool injury list was also playing its part on that November afternoon. Callaghan and Evans were out with cartilage problems, Bobby Graham had a broken ankle and the 'flying winger' Peter Thompson, had

Over the years there have been some fine local derbies played between Liverpool and Everton. There have also been some dull, dour clashes between the two clubs - when over-anticipation by both sides has led to disappointment.

But this game, the 103rd League meeting between The Reds and The Blues, was to prove one of the best.

Everton were the reigning League Champions. Liverpool had last won the title four years earlier, in 1965-66. Since then they had always been serious contenders, always bubbling under the surface of greatness.

Manager Bill Shankly was in the process of rebuilding his team after

Alan Whittle opened the scoring for Everton.

failed a fitness test.

Everton's line-up included three England internationals who had gone to the 1970 World Cup Finals in Mexico - Alan Ball, Tommy Wright and Brian Labone.

The first half gave little indication of what was to come. After 45 minutes the teams trooped into the Anfield tunnel with the score line at 0-0, Everton having enjoyed a marginal advantage. In truth the game had so far been dominated by the edginess and nerves so typical of a local derby. And when the teams ran out again for the second half, the spectators could have been forgiven for expecting the game to end in stalemate.

However, in the 56th minute, the game was transformed - and the true spirit of soccer was released. It happened when Liverpool's captain Tommy Smith attempted to dribble the ball out of defence. He then hit an uncharacteristically bad pass across his own penalty area. This fluff was immediately seized upon by Everton striker Alan Whittle who clipped the ball over Clemence in the Liverpool goal. The score now: 1-0 to Everton.

Eight minutes later the Liverpool defence hesitated, expecting an offside decision to come from the linesman following a through ball from Alan Ball. The linesman's flag stayed down and the ball fell to Everton winger Morrisey who provided centre-forward Joe Royle with the opportunity to put the Blues two up.

The League Champions then proceeded to produce a devastating display of football finesse. Alan Ball in particular was quite stunning, teasing the Liverpool defence and threatening a possible goal rout.

Liverpool brought on substitute Phil Boersma, a speedy forward, in place of the inexperienced John McLaughlin, while Everton had already substituted the injured Howard Kendall with Keith Newton. The subsequent positional alterations on the pitch made all the difference to the course of the game and created avenues of approach for Liverpool where before there had been none.

Liverpool's first goal came in the 69th minute, when Steve Heighway latched onto a ball on the left and then jinked it through the Everton defence before fooling 'keeper Rankin with a disguised shot.

Liverpool were given new life -

The two captains, Emlyn Hughes and Brian Labone lead the teams out.

and seven minutes later they equalised, when John Toshack headed a superb goal following another Steve Heighway breakthrough.

Eight minutes later, left back Alec Lindsay joined the attack and provided a fine cross into the Everton penalty area. Toshack leapt to meet the ball with his head. He flicked the pass on to right back Chris Lawler who had also joined the attack.

Lawler fired in a shot which beat Rankin. The score: 3-2.

Despite a concerted effort by Everton, Liverpool managed to hang on to their slender lead until the final whistle.

Later Bill Shankly proclaimed: "I have never been prouder of a Liverpool team than I was in this match." He knew then, that his young players would do well in the future.

Liverpool:
Clemence, Lawler, Lindsay, Smith, Lloyd, Hughes, Hall, McLaughlin (sub Boersma), Heighway, Toshack, Ross.

Everton:
Rankin, Wright, Newton (H), Kendall (sub Newton (K)), Labone, Harvey, Whittle, Ball, Royle, Hurst, Morrisey.

Final Score:
LIVERPOOL 3 - EVERTON 2

GREAT GAMES 4

LIVERPOOL V. NEWCASTLE UNITED

FA Cup Final
Played at Wembley Stadium
4th May, 1974

Nine years after winning their first ever FA Cup Final, and three years after finishing as Runners-up to Arsenal, Liverpool were back again for their fifth crack at the trophy.

Their Wembley opponents on this occasion were Newcastle United, a team studded with brilliant individual

A moment of contemplation for Newcastle's Malcolm MacDonald during a break in play.

players. Among them was striker Malcolm MacDonald (known as 'SuperMac' wherever he played), Kenny Hibbitt, John Tudor, Bobby Moncur, Willie McFaul, and two players who would eventually star in the red shirts of Liverpool, Terry McDermott and Alan Kennedy.

The Magpies were making their record eleventh appearance in an FA Cup Final. If they won the match it would mean yet another record, that of seven FA Cup Final victories.

The first half of the game proved a ragged affair with the advantage only slightly in Liverpool's favour - and the teams went into the dressing rooms at half time with the score line at 0-0.

After 51 minutes Alec Lindsay put the ball into The Magpies' net, only to be ruled offside by referee Kew. Seven minutes later Kevin Keegan latched onto a Tommy Smith centre, brought the ball swiftly under control then volleyed it past McFaul for Liverpool's opener.

In the 75th minute John Toshack back-heeled the ball on to Steve Heighway who finished the job by heading The Reds' second goal of the afternoon.

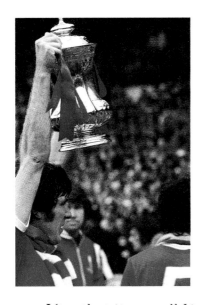

After that it was all Liverpool, as the team provided a fine display of one-sided soccer. Under instructions from manager Bill Shankly, they played some superb possession passing, and in the 88th minute a twelve pass move beginning with goalkeeper Ray Clemence, ended in Keegan's second goal of the game.

Liverpool had won the Cup for the second time in their history.

Next day the gentlemen of the Press were unanimous in their praise of The Reds' performance. One newspaper called it 'the most one-sided final since 1960' (when Wolves had trounced Blackburn Rovers 3-0).

Back on Merseyside the victorious team were greeted by some 250,000 fans, all eager for a glimpse of the trophy, and of manager Bill Shankly.

Little did they know that within two months of the Wembley triumph 'Shanks' would announce his retirement from the game.

Liverpool:
Clemence, Smith, Lindsay, Thompson, Cormack, Hughes, Keegan, Hall, Heighway, Toshack, Callaghan.

Newcastle United:
McFaul, Clarke, Kennedy, McDermott, Howard, Moncur, Cassidy, Smith (sub Gibbs), MacDonald, Tudor, Hibbitt.

Final Score:
LIVERPOOL 3 - NEWCASTLE UNITED 0

Above left: Liverpool's captain, Emlyn Hughes, holds the cup aloft. Right: Liverpool's two goal hero, Kevin Keegan in action and below: The Liverpool players celebrate their win

Bill Shankly became one of football's most illustrious managers and the driving force and inspiration behind Liverpool's modern success.

He was born in Glenbuck, Ayrshire, the second youngest in a family of ten children.

His football career began as a player with Carlisle United in 1932. The following year saw him move to Second Division Preston North End in a £500 transfer deal. In 1933-34 Shankly played at right half for Preston as they headed for promotion (finishing as Runners-up to Grimsby).

While with Preston, 'Shanks' appeared in two FA Cup Finals, and gained a winner's medal in 1938 when the club beat Huddersfield Town 1-0 after extra time at Wembley. He remained at Deepdale until ending his playing career in 1949.

Bill Shankly then turned to management. First with his debut club, Carlisle United and later with Grimsby, Workington and Huddersfield Town (for whom he signed the phenomenal Denis Law).

But it was with Liverpool that Shanks was to make his greatest mark on football history. He became manager at Anfield in December 1959 when the club were in the Second Division.

SHANKS
-THE FATHER OF MODERN LIVERPOOL

He then began a massive rebuilding programme involving the release of no less than 24 players from Liverpool's books and then investing wisely in the transfer market.

Among the players signed by Shankly in his first years at Anfield were towering defender Ron Yeats from Dundee United, centre-forward Ian St. John from Motherwell and Gordon Milne, a stylish midfielder from Shankly's old club, Preston.

Meanwhile, he was also nurturing the talents of a number of home grown players; Roger Hunt (destined to become the club's leading goalscorer), Gerry Byrne, Jimmy Melia and Ian Callaghan (destined to become the club's most faithful servant).

Under Shankly's astute leadership, Liverpool won the Second Division

Championship in 1962 (41 goals were scored by Roger Hunt in that campaign). And that proved to be the beginnings of modern Liverpool.

Shanks was destined to lead The Reds to three League Championships; in 1963-64, 1965-66 and 1972-73; to two FA Cup Final victories; 1965 and 1974, and to the club's first European triumph: the UEFA Cup in 1972-73.

Following the 3-0 drubbing of Newcastle in the 1974 Cup Final, Bill Shankly announced his retirement from the game.

The world of football and the Liverpool faithful in particular were stunned by the news. It was as if they had expected Shankly to go on forever. How, they wondered, could Anfield possibly survive without him?

But such was the strength that Shanks had built into the backbone of the club, that his successor, Bob Paisley, would lead the club to even greater heights.

Shanks settled into a well deserved retirement. He wrote an autobiography which was published in 1976, and he was often asked his opinions on various football matters.

In September 1981, Bill Shankly OBE, suffered a heart attack and later died in hospital.

Above: *Bill Shankly, during his days as manager of Huddersfield Town, coaching some of the club's young players.*

His passing was mourned throughout the world of football. The famous 'Shankly Gates' were erected at Anfield in his memory - adorned by the wrought iron legend 'You'll Never Walk Alone'. A fitting tribute to the man who was 'The Father of Modern Liverpool'.

Bill Shankly announces his retirement.

GREAT GAMES 5

LIVERPOOL v. ST. ETIENNE

European Cup Quarter-Final
(second leg)
Played at Anfield
16th March, 1977.

Bob Paisley was now in charge of things at Anfield. At this time, in the 1976-77 season, Liverpool were chasing the League title. They were still in the FA Cup having reached the sixth round, and they were attempting to reach the European Cup Final.

Opponents St. Etienne, champions of France, had provided something of a setback to Liverpool's Euro ambitions when, in the opening leg of the fixture, they won 1-0. Therefore it was vital that The Reds put up a good display for the return at Anfield.

The atmosphere at Anfield that night has been described as 'electric' - it was certainly enough to shock Liverpool into action. Within two minutes they were a goal ahead. Kevin Keegan scored from 25 yards to make the aggregate score 1-1.

Liverpool increased the pressure in an attempt to find the break-through. But things went drastically wrong for

St. Etienne's Rocheteau receives condolences from Ray Kennedy after the match.

"SuperSub" David Fairclough who scored Liverpool's winner.

than six minutes of the match remaining, he latched onto a Ray Kennedy pass, ran fully forty yards, beat three defenders and then fired a low shot past the St. Etienne 'keeper Curkovic. It was a great goal and one for which David Fairclough will always be remembered at Anfield.

After the match captain Emlyn Hughes described it as, "One of the most exciting," he'd ever played in.

Liverpool were through to the semis.

Liverpool:
Clemence, Neal, Jones, Smith, Kennedy, Hughes, Keegan, Case, Heighway, Toshack (sub Fairclough), Callaghan.

St. Etienne:
Curkovic, Janvion, Farison, Merchadier (sub Revelli H.), Lopez, Bathenay, Rocheteau, Larque, Revelli P., Synaeghel, Santini.

Final Score:
LIVERPOOL 3 - ST. ETIENNE 1

them in the 50th minute when Bathenay equalised for St. Etienne.

In the event of a drawn aggregate score, away goals counted as double. This meant that Liverpool now had to win by two clear goals - surely an impossible task!

Then Ray Kennedy scored for The Reds, with a low drive. But still another goal was needed to ensure a semi-final place for Liverpool.

The French team, sensing victory, were doggedly holding on, and the tension increased with each passing minute.

In the 75th minute, the injured John Toshack limped off the pitch to be replaced by David Fairclough. Fairclough was known as 'Supersub', thanks to his incredible knack of scoring important goals for Liverpool when brought on as 12th man.

Once again young Fairclough was to live up to his nickname. With less

Kevin Keegan who scored from 25 yards.

31

Super Red

Ronnie Whelan

Super Red
Alan Hansen

33

GREAT GAMES 6

LIVERPOOL v. BORUSSIA MOENCHENGLADBACH

European Cup Final
Played at the Olympic Stadium, Rome
25th May, 1977.

Having successfully disposed of the French Champions St. Etienne, in one of the best games in Anfield history, Liverpool proceeded to the 1977 European Cup semi-finals where they met FC Zurich, of Switzerland. These games were something of a one-sided anti-climax after the excitement of the St. Etienne match and Liverpool won through with a 6-1 aggregate.

Their opponents in the Final were Borussia Moenchengladbach, of West Germany.

By this time Liverpool had secured the Football League Championship, but had just failed to win the elusive 'double', loosing to Manchester United in the FA Cup Final - a game which had taken place just four days before the European Cup Final in Rome.

Many Liverpool fans had made their way to the capital of Italy, some beginning their journey from Wembley, immediately after the FA Cup Final. It was later calculated that as many as 30,000 of the Anfield faithful had made the long journey to form a vast blanket of red in the crowd of 57,000. Their trip was to prove well worthwhile.

The opening moves of the game were dominated by Liverpool's surprise tactic of pushing forward - a dangerous scheme to say the least, as Borussia were renowned as one of the best counter-attacking sides in Europe.

Indeed, it looked as if things had gone disastrously wrong when the Germans broke clear early in the match. Bonhof fired a shot which beat Ray Clemence, but then struck the post.

Gradually, however, Liverpool took control of the game. In the 27th minute Steve Heighway jinked his way to the edge of the Borussia penalty area before releasing a delicately weighted pass to the feet of the onrushing Terry McDermott. Terry finished the job by slotting the ball past 'keeper Kneib for Liverpool's first.

In the second half it was Borussia's turn to push forward. In the 51st minute a mistimed back pass by Jimmy Case was seized upon by Simonsen who converted it into Borussia's equaliser.

Then the pressure was really on The Reds - and they clung on for dear life in a ten minute blasting of their penalty area.

After that the scales tipped back in Liverpool's favour. In the 67th minute a Steve Heighway corner was floated

Above: *Terry McDermott and Jimmy Case proudly show off the European Cup.* Below: *Old war horse, Tommy Smith, who scored Liverpool's second goal.*

over the Borussia box - to be met by the head of Tommy Smith, the veteran 'Pool player who had announced that this would be his last game for the club (it wasn't!). Smith's header rocketed into the back of the net.

Victory was well and truly sealed for Liverpool in the 82nd minute when Phil Neal calmly scored from the penalty spot after Kevin Keegan had been upended by Vogts.

Liverpool were Champions of Europe at last.

Borussia Moenchengladbach:
Kneib, Vogts, Klinkhammer, Wittkamp, Bonhof, Wohlers (sub Hannes), Simonsen, Wimmer (sub Kulik), Stielike, Schaeffer, Heynckes.

Liverpool:
Clemence, Neal, Jones, Smith, Kennedy, Hughes, Keegan, Case, Heighway, Callaghan, McDermott.

Final Score:
BORUSSIA MOENCHENGLADBACH 1 - LIVERPOOL 3

SUPER
RED
Steve
Staunton

36

SUPER RED
Gary Ablett

GREAT GAMES 7

LIVERPOOL v. SPURS

League Division One
Played at Anfield
2nd September, 1978.

One of Liverpool's most complete League performances took place at the start of the 1978-79 season. The Reds' victims on this auspicious occasion were Spurs, only recently promoted back to the First Division after a season in the Second.

European Cup holders Liverpool had already won their first three League games of the season. But this, the fourth, was to prove their biggest win of their 11th Championship winning campaign.

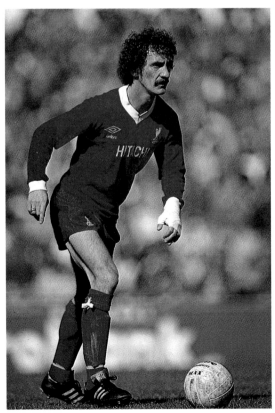

Terry McDermott.

Kenny Dalglish opened Liverpool's account when he scored with a low drive in the 8th minute. 'King' Kenny added a second following a Jimmy Case free kick in the 20th minute.

Eight minutes later Ray Kennedy made it 3-0 to the home side with a superb header from a Terry McDermott cross.

The busiest man on the field was Spurs' goalkeeper Daines. But for his sterling efforts the score might have reached double figures before half time, so forceful and constant were Liverpool's attacks. As it was, the half time score stood at 3-0 to Liverpool.

The second half was just three minutes old when The Reds went further ahead, through substitute David Johnson who scored with a magnificent drive from 15 yards.

Ten minutes later Johnson added Liverpool's fifth goal of the afternoon, following a superb build-up involving Kenny Dalglish and Ray Kennedy. By now Spurs must have been wishing they were on the coach back to White Hart Lane. But there was still more to come!

Liverpool's sixth came from the penalty spot when Steve Heighway was tripped. Phil Neal did the honours.

The 76th minute of the game saw the crowning glory of the afternoon. The ball began well back in Liverpool's half. It was moved swiftly forwards by Ray Kennedy, David Johnson and Steve Heighway. It was then crossed to

Ricardo Villa.

Spurs' far post where it was met by the head of Terry McDermott for Liverpool's seventh. It was a pure team goal which manager Bob Paisley later described as "One of the best in the history of the club."

Despite the combined talents of the Argentinian World Cup stars Ossie Ardiles and Ricardo Villa - and the magic touch of Glenn Hoddle, Spurs had been unable to do anything to contain the power of the Super Reds.

Even at such an early stage in the campaign Liverpool were looking like sure fire Champions.

Ossie Ardiles.

Liverpool:
Clemence, Neal, Kennedy (A), Thompson, Kennedy (R), Hughes (sub Johnson), Dalglish, Case, Heighway, McDermott, Souness.

Tottenham Hotspur:
Daines, McAllister, Naylor, Hoddle, Lacy, Perryman, Villa, Ardiles, Taylor, Duncan, McNab.

Final Score:
**LIVERPOOL 7 -
TOTTENHAM HOTSPUR 0**

Kenny Dalglish.

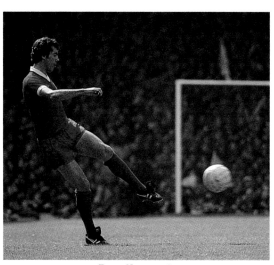

Ray Kennedy.

SUPER RED
Peter Beardsley

SUPER RED
Gary Gillespie

GREAT GAMES 8

LIVERPOOL v. REAL MADRID

European Cup Final
Played at the Parc des Princes, Paris
27th May, 1981.

Twice Liverpool had won the European Cup; in 1977 against Borussia Moenchengladbach, and in 1978 against FC Bruges. Now, 1981 saw them attempting a third victory in the tournament.

Opponents Real Madrid were the most famous football club in Europe and the most successful club in the history of the tournament, having won the trophy no less than six times in eight Final appearances. And so the stage in Paris was set for a fine football match.

In the event, however, the match turned into a dour, physical affair with neither defence giving so much as an inch.

The game did have its moments though: A Laurie Cunningham cross was cut-out by Ray Clemence, Ray Kennedy was booked for a foul on Real 'keeper Agustin, Graeme Souness had a double attempt at goal thwarted by Agustin, Clemence caught a header from Santillana just under the bar. These had been the highlights of the game...until the 82nd minute.

Then, Sammy Lee, about to take a throw-in, had the ball grabbed off him by Ray Kennedy who felt that he could hurl the ball further than little Lee could. Kennedy took the throw and the ball sailed onto the chest of full-back Alan Kennedy, who had made a rare foray into the Spaniards' defence. He controlled it perfectly then darted into the penalty area, successfully riding an attempted tackle by Cortes, before unleashing a well hit left foot shot which beat Agustin and finished up in the back of the Real net. For Liverpool, the remaining eight minutes were simply a matter of holding onto their lead.

The Reds had won their third European Cup Final - and manager Bob Paisley became the first team boss to win a hat-trick of such triumphs.

Captain Phil Thompson in jubliant mood.

Above left: *Alan Kennedy* ... *the game.* Right: *The final score is flashed on to the electronic ⸱* ... *e Liverpool players hug goalscorer Kennedy and .* ... *son with the cup.*

Liverpool:
Clemence, Neal, Kennedy (A), Thompson, Kennedy (R), Hansen, Dalglish (sub Case), Lee, Johnson, McDermott, Souness.

Real Madrid:
Agustin, Garcia, Cortes (sub Pineda), Garcia Navejas, Sabido, Del Bosque, Angel, Camacho, Stielike, Juanito, Santillana, Cunningham.

Final Score:
LIVERPOOL 1 - REAL MADRID 0

LIVERPOOL GOAL GETTERS

Over the years Liverpool has enjoyed the expertise of some great goal getters.

These players scored more than 200 goals for The Reds:

Roger Hunt *(1959-1970)*
285
Gordon Hodson *(1925-1936)*
240
Billy Liddell *(1945-1961)*
229

Roger Hunt.

These players scored more than 100 goals for Liverpool:

Ian Rush *(1980-1987)*
198 *
Kenny Dalglish *(1977-1988)*
168
Henry Chambers *(1919-1928)*
151
Jack Parkinson *(1899-1914)*
128
Sam Raybould *(1899-1907)*
127
Dick Forshaw *(1919-1927)*
124
Ian St. John *(1961-1971)*
118
Jack Balmer *(1935-1952)*
111

Ian Rush.

Above: *Kevin Keegan* and below: *John Toshack.*

These players scored more than 75 goals for Liverpool:

Kevin Keegan *(1971-1977)*
100
John Toshack *(1970-1978)*
95
Albert Stubbins *(1946-1953)*
83
Jack Cox *(1897-1909)*
80
Arthur Goddard *(1901-1914)*
80
Berry Nieuwenhuys *(1933-1947)*
79
David Johnson *(1976-1982)*
78
Jimmy Melia *(1955-1964)*
78
Steve Heighway *(1970-1981)*
76

* *Since rejoining Liverpool in 1988, Ian Rush has passed the magic 200 goals mark.*

GREAT GAMES 9

LIVERPOOL v. A.S. ROMA

European Cup Final
Played at the Olympic Stadium, Rome
30th May, 1984.

By now Joe Fagan had taken over the reins as manager of Liverpool, and in his first season had already secured the Football League Championship and the Milk Cup, thereby following firmly in the footsteps of Shankly and Paisley before him.

But Liverpool were at a definite disadvantage when making their fourth attempt to win the European Cup. The 1984 competition saw their opponents AS Roma playing in the Final on their home ground! As if to add to the difficulties Roma had several world class internationals in their line-up including Falcao and Crezo of Brazil, and Graziani and Conti, two stars of Italy's 1982 World Cup winning team.

Liverpool began the game calmly, playing some finely controlled football. In the 15th minute the ball ran loose as Roma's 'keeper Tancredi fumbled following a challenge by Ronnie Whelan. The ball bobbled crazily about the penalty area - until it was pounced upon by Phil Neal who seized the opportunity to slam it into Roma's net.

For the next 28 minutes it was all Liverpool. Ian Rush almost scored twice and another 'goal' was disallowed for offside. Then, just before half time, the drama increased when Roma equalised with a superbly headed goal by Pruzzo.

The second half was a long, drawn out battle with Liverpool looking slightly the better side. However, after 90 minutes the scores were still level at one-all. Extra time simply continued the stalemate and the game went to penalties.

Steve Nicol fired first - and he missed!

Next on the spot was Roma's skipper Di Bartolemei. He scored. 1-0 to Roma.

So did Phil Neal for The Reds. 1-1.

Then Conti missed for Roma to keep the teams on level terms: 1-1.

Souness scored. Righetti scored: 2-2.

Rush scored. Graziani *missed*: 2-3.

Finally Alan Kennedy sealed the matter by calmly converting his kick: 2-4. Once again he was the hero of the hour. And Liverpool had won their fourth European Cup Final.

AS Roma:
Tancredi, Nappi, Bonetti, Righetti, Falcao, Nela, Conti, Cerezo (sub Strukelj), Pruzzo (sub Chierico), Di Bartolemei, Graziani.

Liverpool:
Grobbelaar, Neal, Kennedy, Lawrenson, Whelan, Hansen, Dalglish (sub Robinson), Lee, Rush, Johnson (sub Nicol), Souness.

Final Score:
AS ROMA 1 - LIVERPOOL 1
[Liverpool won 4-2 on penalties]

Liverpool's opening goal scored by full-back Phil Neal. Left: He beats A.S. Roma's Falcao to the ball and middle: Shoots for goal as three defenders close in and right: His shot is goal bound.

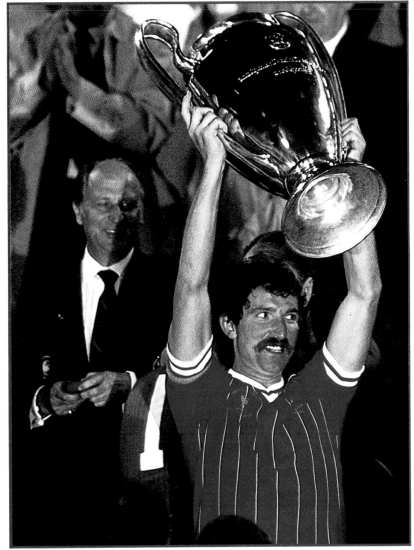

Captain Graeme Souness with the European Cup.

Below: Conti misses and the penalty shoot-out stays at 1-1. Middle: Graziani misses and it's 3-2 to Liverpool. Right: Alan Kennedy slots home the vital penalty winner.

SUPER RED

Bruce Grobbelaar

SUPER
RED
Steve Nicol

49

THE DOUBLE

-A DREAM FULFILLED

In the summer of 1985 Liverpool Football Club announced the retirement of manager Joe Fagan - and the appointment of his successor, Kenny Dalglish.

Many pundits felt that this was a reckless move by the club. For although Dalglish had been an outstanding player for Liverpool, football lore decreed that great players do not necessarily make great managers. The popular opinion was that this could be the beginning of the end for Liverpool.

How wrong can you get?

Kenny Dalglish was to prove the inspiration and driving force behind Liverpool's greatest ever domestic season.

The 1985-86 campaign began with a 2-0 win at home to Arsenal, with goals from Ronnie Whelan and Steve Nicol (this was the first of 26 League victories which would include a 6-0 thrashing of Oxford United, and 5-0

defeats of Ipswich Town, Coventry City and Birmingham City).

In September, Steve McMahon, Kenny Dalglish's first major signing, was recruited into the Anfield Army in a £350,000 transfer deal with Aston Villa. Steve, a tough and talented midfielder, would have a tremendous impact on the team's performance. He scored his first goal for the club on 21st September in a 3-2 victory over local rivals Everton.

Ian Rush was in fine form too. He would become Liverpool's leading scorer that season, with a tally of 22 League goals.

However, by the end of 1985, thanks to a string of disappointing results (two draws and defeats by Arsenal and Manchester City), The Reds had slumped to fourth place in the table.

The FA Cup campaign began in January with a Third Round tie against Norwich City who were then struggling to regain their First Division status. Liverpool won 5-0, with goals from McDonald, Walsh, McMahon, Whelan and Wark.

Stamford Bridge was the venue for the Fourth Round encounter, a televised game against Championship contenders Chelsea. Liverpool took a while to gain control of the match, but eventually won 2-1, with goals by Ian Rush and Mark Lawrenson.

The Fifth Round took The Reds to Bootham Crescent, home of Third Division York City. There, with Kenny Dalglish in the side, they were held to a 1-1 draw, Jan Molby scoring from the penalty spot in the 64th minute. The replay at Anfield was hard work too, the score after 90 minutes was 1-1, Liverpool's goal coming from John Wark. It was only in extra time that the Anfield outfit got the better of plucky York with further goals from Molby and Dalglish, taking them into the Sixth Round.

By then Liverpool's League form had improved somewhat, the only setback being a 1-2 defeat by Ipswich Town.

On 22nd February, 1986, Liverpool played local rivals Everton in the League at Anfield. The Blues won 2-0, and placed a few doubts as to The Reds' ability to win the title. But that was to be the last time Liverpool lost all season.

The Cup campaign continued against Watford. The game, played at Anfield, ended in a frustrating 0-0 draw. The replay, at Vicarage Road, looked likely to end Liverpool's Wembley hopes, with Watford a goal ahead and the final whistle only minutes away. Then Ian Rush was tripped in the Watford box. The penalty was expertly converted by Jan Molby and the game went into extra time.

Once again Liverpool piled on the pressure in the remaining 30 minutes. This time Ian Rush scored the winner.

In the semi-final Liverpool met Southampton, at neutral White Hart Lane. Again the game went into extra time, with the score at 0-0. Again Ian

Opposite page: Player-manager, Kenny Dalglish proudly shows off the FA Cup and League Championmship Trophy. *Above:* Dalglish after scoring the only goal of Liverpool's game against Chelsea, which clinched the First Division Championship.

Rush proved Liverpool's saviour with goals in the 99th and 108th minutes.

The Reds were in the FA Cup Final for the seventh time in their history. Their opponents would be fellow Merseysiders, Everton - the toughest side they had faced all season.

Meanwhile, the race for the League Championship was hotting-up. It gradually narrowed to a three team contest between Liverpool, Everton and West Ham United.

It became the closest closing campaign in years, and it went right down to the bare bones of the last games of the season. If Liverpool could defeat Chelsea at Stamford Bridge, then they would win the title and be assured of a crack at the elusive 'double'.

Fittingly, it was Kenny Dalglish who scored the only goal of the game, in the 23rd minute.

Liverpool were Champions for the 16th time - and the 'double' was a distinct possibility.

All that The Reds of Anfield had to do was beat The Blues of Goodison Park, at Wembley...

THE DOUBLE
-A DREAM FULFILLED

LIVERPOOL v. EVERTON

FA Cup Final
Played at Wembley Stadium
10th May, 1986.

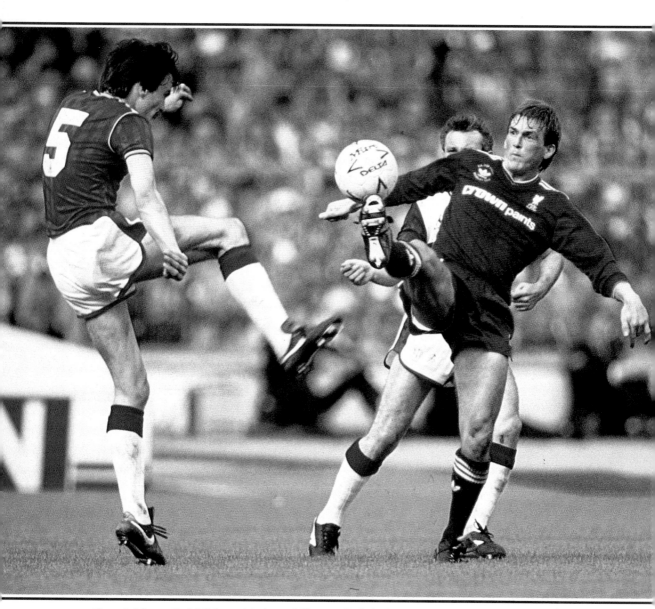

Derek Mountfield (blue shirt) and Kenny Dalglish in action during the game.

Only four teams had 'done the double' in the history of English football; Preston North End in 1888-89, Aston Villa in 1896-97, Tottenham Hotspur in 1960-61 and Arsenal in 1970-71. Others had tried; Manchester United, Sunderland, Newcastle United, Everton, and Liverpool themselves. So, on this occasion, the weight of history and the scales of likelihood were tipped towards Everton.

Everton had finished the season as League Runners-up to Liverpool and had no intention of finishing as second best in the Cup Final.

These then, were the ingredients of the drama which made the first Merseyside Cup Final such a great talking point, not only in the city of Liverpool, but all over the country.

The Final was played under a cloudless blue sky. And it was the Blue of Everton which showed itself first - with a goal in the 28th minute from the 1986 Footballer of the Year, Gary Lineker.

Lineker, Everton's goalscorer, tussles with Liverpool's Mark Lawrenson.

Gary Lineker opens the scoring for Everton.

For the next half hour Everton seemed to contain Liverpool. And it looked as if another 'double' dream was destined to bite the dust.

Suddenly Liverpool defender Jim Beglin seized on a poor pass from Everton's full back Stevens. Beglin slipped the ball to Jan Molby who in turn played a simple ball forward into the path of Ian Rush.

Rush, the quickest goalscorer in modern football, fired in a hard shot which beat Bobby Mimms in the Everton goalmouth: one-all.

Everton almost pulled ahead again, but Graham Sharp's header was miraculously touched over the crossbar by Bruce Grobbelaar.

In the 63rd minute, a fine move involving Rush and Molby, was converted by the unmarked Craig

Craig Johnston watches his shot beat Mimms in the Everton goal to send Liverpool 2-1 up.

Johnston who side-footed Liverpool's second from close range.

Ian Rush made certain of the matter when, in the 84th minute, he cracked the ball past Bobby Mimms following a delicately chipped pass from Ronnie Whelan.

It had been a great game. It was Liverpool's game. It was Liverpool's 'double'.

Ian Rush scores his second and Liverpool's third.

Everton:
Mimms, Stevens (sub Heath), Van Den Hauwe, Ratcliffe, Mountfield, Reid, Steven, Lineker, Sharp, Bracewell, Sheedy.

Liverpool:
Grobbelaar, Lawrenson, Beglin, Nicol, Whelan, Hansen, Dalglish, Johnston, Rush, Molby, MacDonald.

Final Score:
EVERTON 1 - LIVERPOOL 3

Rush side-steps Bobby Mimms and scores Liverpool's equaliser.

SUPER
RED
Steve
McMahon

WORD SEARCH

The names if 16 Liverpool stars are hidden in the grid below. Using a pen or pencil can you find them all? They may be hidden forwards, backwards, up, down or diagonally - but always in a straight line. (Solution on Page 61).

These are the names to look for..

IAN RUSH
BRUCE GROBBELAAR
RAY HOUGHTON
GARY ABLETT
JOHN BARNES
MIKE HOOPER
PETER BEARDSLEY
GARY GILLESPIE
STEVE MCMAHON
ALAN HANSEN
KENNY DALGLISH
RONNIE WHELAN
JIM BEGLIN
BARRY VENISON
JAN MOLBY
KEVIN MACDONALD

B	R	U	C	E	G	R	O	B	B	E	L	A	A	R
I	Y	W	L	I	A	W	Z	M	N	A	O	P	O	A
A	V	I	V	S	T	L	O	V	P	F	H	N	I	Y
N	P	T	Z	Y	G	U	A	Q	B	L	F	V	M	H
R	E	E	G	S	W	J	A	N	M	O	L	B	Y	O
U	T	A	W	U	T	J	M	G	H	X	N	X	L	U
S	E	Z	W	S	R	P	B	I	F	A	T	J	K	G
H	R	B	R	H	E	A	S	H	E	H	N	I	R	H
X	B	A	B	A	X	P	A	Q	H	Q	K	S	K	T
Y	E	R	S	E	N	R	A	B	N	H	O	J	E	O
G	A	R	Y	A	B	L	E	T	T	F	F	O	G	N
A	R	Y	V	B	C	C	E	F	P	M	O	P	G	O
R	D	V	N	A	L	E	H	W	E	I	N	N	O	R
Y	S	E	T	K	M	E	L	W	Z	M	B	A	B	N
G	L	N	I	Q	D	R	Z	F	C	N	O	L	N	D
I	E	I	M	I	K	E	H	O	O	P	E	R	S	J
L	Y	S	Q	C	J	I	M	B	E	G	L	I	N	A
L	X	O	V	D	X	C	L	O	S	K	E	Z	O	V
E	Y	N	U	E	L	V	B	L	P	N	L	G	Y	R
S	T	E	V	E	M	C	M	A	H	O	N	E	O	Q
P	D	J	C	U	A	A	W	Y	T	X	B	M	Z	N
I	D	L	A	N	O	D	C	A	M	N	I	V	E	K
E	K	E	N	N	Y	D	A	L	G	L	I	S	H	B

GREAT GAMES 10

LIVERPOOL v. NOTTINGHAM FOREST

Football League Division One
Played at Anfield
13th April, 1988.

John Barnes (red shirt) had a superb game against Forest.

This was the game which prompted the legendary Tom Finney to declare, "Liverpool must be the greatest team of all time."

Certainly The Reds had performed magnificently throughout the 1987-88 season - which would eventually see them as Champions for the 17th time. During the course of the campaign they had equalled the fourteen year old First Division record held by Leeds United, of 29 League games without defeat from the start of the season.

En route they had recorded some impressive victories and put on display after display of flowing, elegant football. This was due in part to the arrival in the team of two soccer artists: England internationals Peter Beardsley and John Barnes. (At the close of the season Barnes would find himself voted Footballer of the Year.)

Liverpool would go all the way to Wembley as well in '87-88. In fact they looked certainties to pull off the 'double' for the second time in three seasons. But it was not to be. Wimbledon saw to that, thanks to Lawrie Sanchez's goal and Dave Beasant's penalty save.

Ray Houghton got Liverpool's first.

Nottingham Forest had fallen victims to Liverpool in the semi-final of the FA Cup on 9th April. However, they had also been only the second team to beat The Reds in the League (Everton had been the first, calling a halt to Liverpool's record-breaking attempt). If Forest thought they could repeat the feat at Anfield, they were in for a great big shock, for this game was to prove the pinnacle of a great season for Liverpool.

Each and every player in the team performed magnificently that day, and they were compared afterwards to the great Real Madrid side which had once dominated Europe, with the likes of Puskas, Kopa, Gento and Di Stefano.

Ray Houghton opened the scoring following a pass from John Barnes in the 18th minute. John Aldridge hit Liverpool's second after 26 minutes - his strike coming from a 30 yard defence-splitting pass delivered by Peter Beardsley.

In the second half defender Gary Gillespie added The Reds' third with a well directed volley from 12 yards out. Once again the provider was Beardsley.

In the 78th minute John Barnes, enjoying himself on the left, cheekily slipped the ball between Chettle's

legs, beat Crosby and then knocked the ball into the path of Beardsley, who deservedly got his name onto the score sheet with Liverpool's fourth goal of the evening.

John Aldridge scored Liverpool's fifth, in the 88th minute.

All in all it had been a textbook display of total teamwork, footballing sense and the application of marvellous soccer skills. It was, according to Tom Finney, "the finest exhibition I have seen by any team in all my time of playing and watching the game."

Liverpool:

Grobbelaar, Gillespie, Ablett, Nicol, Spackman, Beardsley, Aldridge, Houghton (sub Johnston), Barnes, McMahon (sub Molby).

Nottingham Forest:

Sutton, Chettle, Pearce, Walker (sub Wassell), Foster, Wilson, Crosby, Webb, Clough, Glover, Rice.

Final Score:
LIVERPOOL 5 - NOTTINGHAM FOREST 0

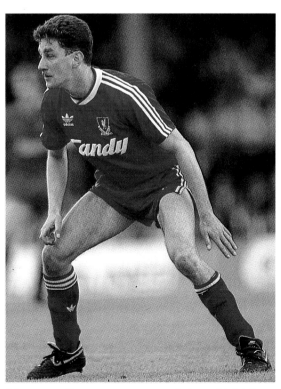

Liverpool's top scorer, John Aldridge, helped himself to two goals.

SUPER RED

Ray Houghton

60

QUIZ

1. With which club did Mike Hooper begin his goalkeeping career?

2. Liverpool paid £750,000 for the services of John Aldridge, to which club?

3. To which club did Nigel Spackman transfer in February 1989?

4. Liverpool paid £800,000 for the services of Ray Houghton, to which club?

5. For which country does Ronnie Whelan play?

6. Which Canadian club did Peter Beardsley once play for?

7. Who scored the winning goal in the 1988 FA Cup Final?

8. With which club did Steve McMahon begin his career?

9. With which club did Gary Gillespie begin his career?

10. Who occupied the manager's chair at Anfield before Kenny Dalglish took over?

11. In which year did Liverpool first win the FA Cup?

12. In which season did Liverpool first win the Football League Championship?

13. How many times have Liverpool won the European Cup?

14. From which club did John Barnes transfer to Liverpool?

15. Whose record of unbeaten First Division games did Liverpool equal in 1987-88?

WORD SEARCH ANSWERS

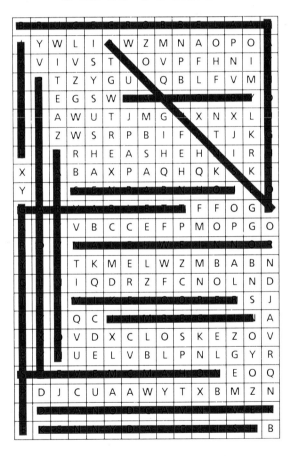

ANSWERS